A Little Monster's
GUIDE TO CONFIDENCE

T0385228

A LITTLE MONSTER'S GUIDE TO CONFIDENCE

Copyright © Emily Snape, 2024

All illustrations by Emily Snape

All rights reserved.

No part of this book may be reproduced by any means, nor transmitted, nor translated into a machine language, without the written permission of the publishers.

Emily Snape has asserted her right to be identified as the author of this work in accordance with sections 77 and 78 of the Copyright, Designs and Patents Act 1988.

Condition of Sale
This book is sold subject to the condition that it shall not, by way of trade or otherwise, be lent, resold, hired out or otherwise circulated in any form of binding or cover other than that in which it is published and without a similar condition including this condition being imposed on the subsequent purchaser.

An Hachette UK Company
www.hachette.co.uk

Vie Books, an imprint of Summersdale Publishers
Part of Octopus Publishing Group Limited
Carmelite House
50 Victoria Embankment
LONDON
EC4Y 0DZ
UK

www.summersdale.com

Printed and bound in China

ISBN: 978-1-83799-209-6

Substantial discounts on bulk quantities of Summersdale books are available to corporations, professional associations and other organizations. For details contact general enquiries: telephone: +44 (0) 1243 771107 or email: enquiries@summersdale.com.

Neither the author nor the publisher can be held responsible for any loss or claim arising out of the use, or misuse, of the suggestions made herein. None of the views or suggestions in this book are intended to replace medical opinion from a doctor. If you have concerns about your health or that of a child in your care, please seek advice from a medical professional.

A Little Monster's
GUIDE TO CONFIDENCE

Emily Snape

vie

Note to parents and carers

This book will help your child to:

- Find out what it means to be confident.

- Not compare themselves to others and learn that we all pick things up at our own pace.

- Set acheivable goals and build confidence.

- Use positive self-talk.

- Not be afraid to try new things and learn from mistakes.

- Understand that encouraging and helping others will make them feel more powerful.

These approaches can become tools that will enable your child to feel more confident and secure in themselves.

Oh, hi! I'm Flint. What's your name? This is my little brother, Pip. Pip can feel a bit shy when he meets new people but, like I told him, you look really friendly!

Some monsters can chat to anyone. They make it seem easy, but Pip can get VERY nervous and he rolls up into a ball. I think Pip would feel better if he worked on his CONFIDENCE.

What is CONFIDENCE, Flint?

Hmmmm. Why don't you ask your friends?

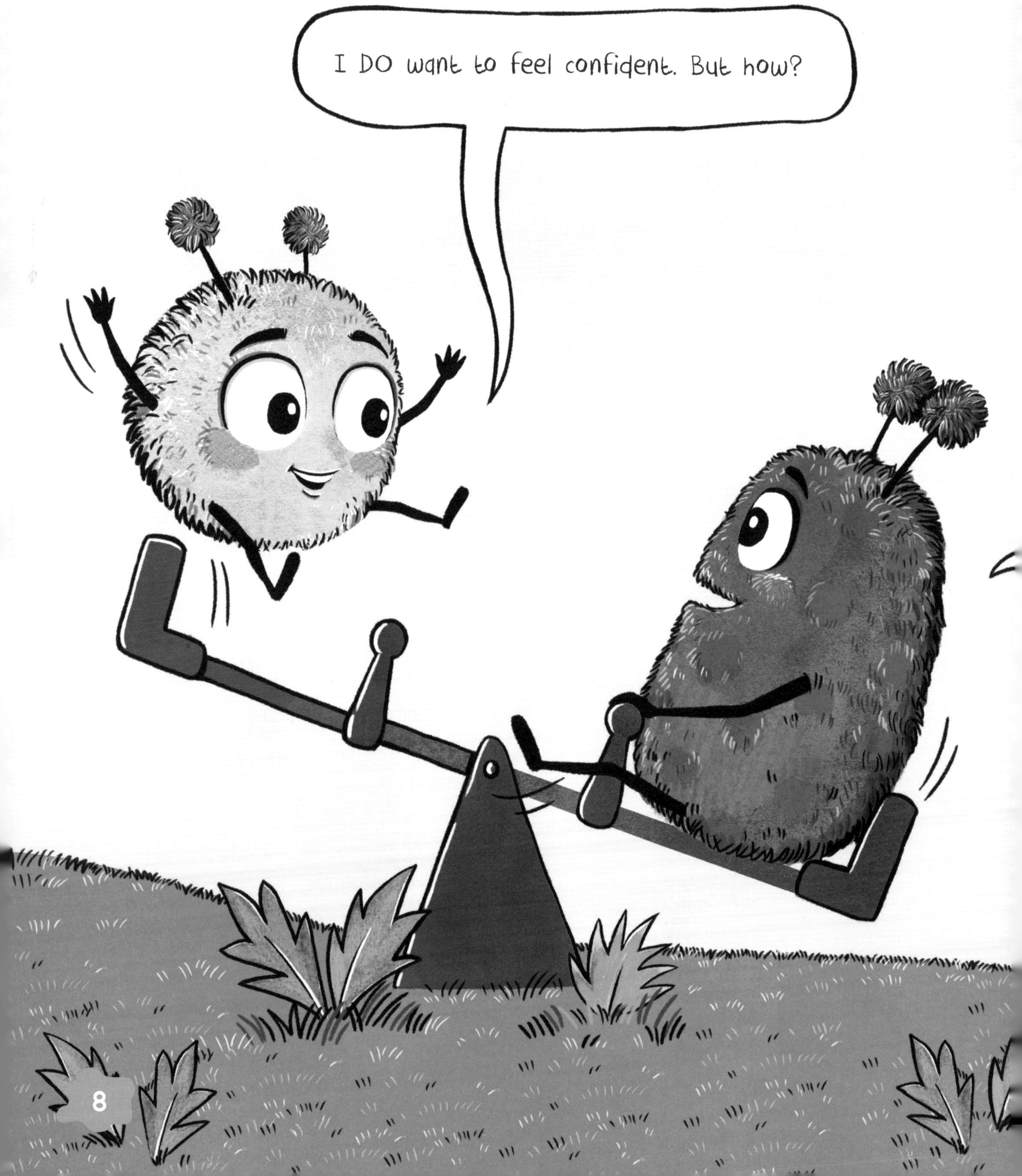
I DO want to feel confident. But how?

We have about 6,000 thoughts a day and it's likely that some of them will be negative. We need to make sure we aren't putting ourselves down. It can really damage our confidence.

If you do notice yourself thinking negatively, remind yourself:

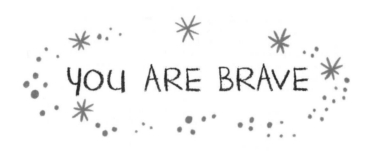

YOU ARE BRAVE

YOU CAN DO IT

And if something goes wrong,
YOU CAN DO BETTER NEXT TIME!

It is important to remember that EVERYBODY is different and learns to do things at different paces.

We all have talents and skills but we also all find some things tricky, and that's okay. Being different is what makes the world interesting and everybody in it special!

I'm great at howling at the moon but I find it difficult to read. I'm working on it!

I feel really confident about my spooking skills but I have to try extra hard at maths.

My brother, Flint, told me what makes him feel confident is knowing he can make a difference.

Helping others and being kind makes him feel valuable.

Flint has organized a sponsored BIG BIKE RIDE around the park to raise money for our school.

I REALLY want to take part... But I can't.

Join the sponsored
BIG BIKE RIDE

Gooberry Park
Saturday
Raise money for Spooking School

So, I spent the day in the park, working on finding my balance, falling off my bike, then getting on and trying again!

Flint explained that mistakes and failures are REALLY important because you can learn from them.

After another few days of working hard, I AM getting better! I try not to compare myself to others - I am improving at my own rate.

We even had slug sandwiches to celebrate. YUM!

While we walked home, Flint explained that it's great to have dreams and goals as they can help build your confidence and give you challenges to work towards.

I've decided I want to be a PROFESSIONAL CYCLIST and WIN a GOLD MEDAL at the OLYMPICS!

Today was the BIG BIKE RIDE around the park...

I was confident. I had worked really hard and I was ready!

Everyone was there to cheer us on.

I took a BIG swig of frog's vomit, got on my bike and started pedalling really fast. It felt GREAT!

But then, I suddenly rode over a spiky rock and my tyre got a puncture!

I couldn't believe it. I wasn't going to be able to complete the course.

Cal offered me his bike, but I wasn't sure if I could ride it. It was a lot bigger than mine.

So I did, and I managed to do the whole lap of the park. I felt so proud of myself. I had done it!

I thanked Cal, then Flint and I had ice cream slugdaes at the cafe.

It was the best day ever!

I am so glad that I tried and didn't give up even when completing the BIG BIKE RIDE seemed impossible.

Slimy Swamp Gala

Come and join in!
31 October

I've decided to organize a new event, a slimy swamp-swimming gala, and I hope everyone will get involved. (I just have to learn how to swim first.)

You've been so kind listening and letting me share my story. I feel much less shy now. Thank you.

And remember, if I can feel confident, so can you!

All you need to do is...

Dare to dream.

Try new things.

Learn from mistakes.

Know that it's OKAY not to be perfect.

We are all unique and that is BRILLIANT!

Hope to see you at the swamp!

About the Author

Emily Snape is a children's author and illustrator living in London. Her work has appeared online, on television, in shops and even on buses! She loves coffee and notebooks, and has three cheeky children, Leo, Fin and Flo, who keep her on her toes and give her lots of inspiration for stories.

You can find out her latest publishing news on Instagram at **@emily_snape_illustrator**.

If you're interested in finding out more about our books, find us on Facebook at **Summersdale Publishers**, on Twitter/X at **@Summersdale** and on Instagram and TikTok at **@summersdalebooks** and get in touch.

We'd love to hear from you!

Thanks very much for buying this Summersdale book.

www.summersdale.com